VICTORIAN BRADFORD

THE LIVING PAST

Titles of related interest from Ryburn Publishing:
The Ryburn Map of Victorian Bradford by Elvira Willmott (1987)
A History of Bradford by David James (1988)

VICTORIAN BRADFORD

THE LIVING PAST

Photographs by

IAN BEESLEY

Printed in Duotone

Introduction and Commentary by

DAVID JAMES

Ryburn Publishing

First published in 1987
by Ryburn Publishing Ltd
Krumlin, Halifax, England

Printed and bound by
Netherwood Dalton & Co Ltd
Bradley Mills, Huddersfield, England

ISBN 1-85331-003-4

Introduction

The nineteenth century historian William Scruton described late eighteenth century Bradford as 'a small rural town, surrounded by green fields and quiet country lanes'. In 1801 it had just over 13,000 inhabitants. Fifty years later it was the seventh largest and fastest growing urban centre in England with a population that had increased by 50% every decade since 1800 and now numbered over 100,000.

This phenomenal growth was due to the mechanisation of the worsted trade: by the middle of the century Bradford was the worsted textile capital of the world. There were 129 mills in the town and neighbourhood and the old methods of hand production had nearly died out, with spinning largely mechanised by 1820 and combing by 1850.

Three developments confirmed Bradford's pre-eminence. First, the trade developed a specialised type of product — a stiff, lustrous, fibre worsted ideally suited for women's dress goods. Secondly, the town became the merchanting centre for the West Riding textile industry, the most famous merchants coming from the German community which had the warehousing district of Little Germany named after it. Thirdly, a dyeing industry was created: Ripley's dye works in Bowling eventually became the largest piece dyeworks in the world.

In human terms the cost of this change from country town to industrial giant was enormous. The town's population consisted largely of immigrants and strangers living in appalling urban squalor. The Morning Chronicle recorded that Bradford was 'an accumulation of mean streets, steep lanes and huge mills, intersected here and there by odious patches of black, muddy waste ground rooted up by pigs and strewn with oyster shells, cabbage stalks and such garbage.'

Effluent was discharged into the local streams or the canal, which acquired the nickname River Stink; drinking water was sometimes unobtainable and often polluted, and the smoke from the factory chimneys filled the air with a thick smog. For many ordinary people, living accommodation was restricted to a single room which in some cases was also used as a workplace. Crime was endemic and drink and violence were often the main social pleasures. Little wonder then that the town frequently erupted into riot and occasionally teetered on the verge of insurrection. It was clear by 1850 that the physical, social and moral environment had to be improved.

In 1847 the town became a borough and the council attempted to provide a framework for a civilised urban life. The police force tackled the problem of crime, the water supply was improved and a new sewage system was started. There were even attempts, albeit not very successful, to curb the pollution of the atmosphere.

The 1860's saw the start of extensive re-building which destroyed the old town and created the Victorian city recorded in this book. The doctrine of civic pride, enthusiastically embraced by the textile barons, resulted in such buildings as the Wool Exchange, St George's Hall and the Town Hall. A beautiful sandstone was locally available and widely used.

The vexed question of where to bury the dead was solved with similar vigour by the formation of the Undercliffe Cemetery Company which acquired a magnificent site to lay out one of the most impressive burial grounds in the United Kingdom.

While these improvements were taking place the worsted trade remained the economic backbone of the town. The years 1850-1870 were the high point of the Bradford worsted trade; the good times came to an end in 1875 when fierce foreign competition and greater protectionism in traditional markets made exports difficult. Furthermore, the trade had neglected the increasing importance of fashion and design. These difficulties led to a restructuring of the industry and the great integrated mills such as Salts, Listers and Black Dyke at Queensbury slowly became uneconomic. The trade grew more specialised and fragmented, and commissioned working, with its lower overheads, became commonplace. Nevertheless, worsteds continued to be by far the biggest local employer and the decline was by no means uniform. Fortunes could still be made, though not as easily as before.

Introduction

The town continued to expand. In 1881 the population was 183,082 and by 1911 it was 288,458. However, after 1870 the local birth rate fell from well above the national average to well below it, and after 1881 real population growth almost ceased. The later increases in population were due largely to extensions of the municipal boundaries: Allerton, Heaton, Thornbury and Tyersal were added in 1882, and Idle, Eccleshill, Thornton, North Bierley and Tong in 1899.

After 1870 the Council earned a reputation for municipal achievement. The nucleus of a public health department was formed with the appointment of a Medical Officer of Health, a Public Analyst, Inspectors of Meat and Slaughter Houses and a Nuisances Inspector. The privately owned gas company was bought in 1871, the canal was drained, and a tramways system was developed, enabling people to live outside the town centre. In 1899 the borough became the first in the country to undertake the supply of electricity. Parks were opened, libraries and museums established and educational responsibilities shouldered. A start was made on council house building. In 1897 the borough was granted city status and it was cited in a contemporary book as a leading example of civic enterprise because of its 'vigorous and enlightened muncipal policy.'

The quality of life improved in other ways. There was a wider choice of leisure activities. Pubs became more elaborate and pleasant. Music halls and theatres were increasingly popular and cinemas too by the end of the period. Cycling and walking became crazes in the 1890's and 1900's; roller skating rinks were opened. Most important of all was football which became an important spectator sport, climaxing in 1911 when Bradford City won the F.A. Cup.

The years before 1914 were Bradford's Indian Summer, the 'last majestic flowering of nineteenth century provincial life'. J.B.Priestley summed up this proud provincialism in commenting, 'What came to an end during the First War — at least in my experience — was a kind of regional self sufficiency, not defying London, but genuinely indifferent to it.' This book celebrates the buildings built during Bradford's Victorian hey-day and illustrates that combination of confidence and civic pride which helped to make it one of the great cities of Victorian England.

Acknowledgements

Many individuals and institutions have helped make this book possible. In particular, thanks must be given to the staff of the West Yorkshire Archive Service, especially Judith Elenor, Lorraine Mackenzie, Christopher Marsden, Ian Mason and Gina Szekeley of the Bradford Office. Elvira Willmott, Carol Greenwood and the other staff of the Reference Department of Bradford Central Library have been extremely helpful. The works of many local historians have been invaluable. Bradford has been lucky in its researchers in recent years and we have benefited enormously from the articles, books and theses which have illuminated the history of the town. The works of John Ayers, Paul Jennings, Derek Linstrum, Geoff Mellor and John Roberts have been particularly useful.

Our thanks are also due to Ilford Ltd for their generous support and to the National Museum of Photography, Film and Television.Finally, we wish to thank Ryburn Publishing for their commitment to this project which they developed and superintended.

Note

Would readers please note that in this book the term Victorian has been used somewhat loosely to include the period until 1914.

The Photographs

City Hall (Photograph number 1)
Banqueting Hall, City Hall extension (2)
Wool Exchange (3 and 4)
Telegraph & Argus (5)
St George's Hall and the Victoria Hotel (6)
Theatre Royal (7)
Alhambra Theatre (8 and 9)
Old Post Office (10 and 11)
National Westminster Bank (12)
Yorkshire Penny Bank (13)
Bradford and Ilkley Community College:
    Alexandra Annexe (14 and 15)
Midland Hotel (16)
Registry Office (17)
Law Russell (18)
Devere House (19)
Austral House (20)
Little Germany (21)
Lister's Mill (22)
Buttershaw Mill (23)
New Mill, Saltaire (24)
Albert Terrace, Saltaire, and Saltaire Mill (25)
Bolton Road warehouses (26)
Black Dyke Mills (27)
Preston Street Landscapes:
    City Road Goods Yard and Alston Works (28-31)
Back-to-back housing (32)
Terraced housing (33)
Semi-detached housing (34)
Bradford Tradesmens Homes (35)
St Luke's Hospital (36)
Rimmington's (37)
Gray's Fisheries (38)
Dudley Hill Picture House (39)
Cock and Bottle (40)
Moulders Arms (41-44)
Cartwright Hall (45)
Bradford and Ilkley Community College:
    Old Building (46)
University of Bradford Management Centre (47)
Bowling Back Lane Board School (48)
Pollard Park Middle School (49)
St John's Church (50)
All Saints' Church (51)
Sion Baptist Chapel (52)
Sheikhs Restaurant (53)
Eastbrook Hall (54)
Undercliffe Cemetery (55-65)

An alphabetical index of the photographs appears at the end of the book. As far as possible, in the captions accompanying the photographs we have given each building the name most likely to help a visitor find it, the address, the architects and the year of opening.

1. City Hall (Market Street; Lockwood and Mawson,1873)

Bradford became a borough in 1847 but twenty years passed before the council decided to build a Town Hall to house its meetings, mayoral functions and municipal departments. It thus lagged well behind nearby Leeds (Brodrick, 1858) and Halifax (Barry, 1863), although regionally it had helped establish the trend of architectural civic grandeur with St George's Hall (Lockwood and Mawson, 1853). Lockwood and Mawson's Gothic design for the Town Hall was chosen in a competition in which they also submitted Classical elevations to the same plan: a contemporary critic commented that there was "nothing to compare with the completeness of the nineteen drawings, the beauty of their delineation and tinting, or with the number, the size or the richness of their glazed and gilded frames." The foundation stone was laid in August 1870 and the official opening took place in September 1873 to the accompaniment of elaborate celebrations and torrential rain. The building's crowning glory is undoubtedly the 200-foot-high tower modelled on that of the Palazzo Vecchio in Florence.

2. The Banqueting Hall, City Hall extension (Channing Way; Edwards and Shaw, 1909)
Within thirty years of the opening of the Town Hall, the city architect, F.E.P. Edwards, was at work on plans to extend it and invited the distinguished architect Richard Norman Shaw to act as a consultant. The facades of the extension, opened in 1909, cleverly complement those of Lockwood and Mawson. The Banqueting Hall is the setting for many of the City's most important functions and has a number of interesting features. The freestone frieze over the mantel-piece symbolically embodies the idea of progress; above are the Arms of the former Bradford County Borough Council. The stained glass windows relate to prominent Bradford families.

3. The Wool Exchange (Market Street; Lockwood and Mawson, 1867)
Opened at a time when Bradford was developing into a classic Victorian town, the Wool Exchange was designed as a place where men engaged in the combing, spinning, manufacturing, dyeing and merchanting of wool textile goods could meet and trade. For a century the Exchange was the centre of the world wool trade and Bradfordians used to say that on the market days of Monday and Thursday "there was not a single type of wool and hair for which a buyer could not be found on the Change." The pinnacled clock tower stands 150 feet high.

4. The Wool Exchange

The interior of the Exchange is impressively spacious and elaborate, demonstrating the wealth and pride of the nineteenth century textile barons. The lofty hammer beam roof is decorated with wrought iron work, which can also be seen on the staircase and the balcony. The statue is of Richard Cobden, the apostle of free trade, whose treaty with France opened the door to the Continental market. It was presented to the Exchange by an American, George Henry Booth, who was a partner in the Bradford firm of Firth, Booth and Co.

5. The Telegraph & Argus (Hall Ings; Andrews and Delauney, 1853)
One of the first and most splendid of Bradford's great warehouses, the building was erected for merchants Milligan and Forbes as a home trade warehouse. Robert Milligan was the first mayor of Bradford in 1847 and his partner Henry Forbes, also a Liberal nonconformist, was made mayor in 1849. The style is derived from the Italian Renaissance palazzo and reflects Victorian Bradford's self-confident view of itself as the new Florence. The architect of the recent adjoining buildings (Arthur Griffin, 1981) was largely successful in substantially extending the premises in a contemporary style without unduly detracting from the older building.

6. St George's Hall (Hall Ings; Lockwood and Mawson, 1853) and the Victoria Hotel (Bridge Street; Lockwood and Mawson, 1867)

By the late 1840's it was clear that the lack of a major public hall was a considerable inconvenience to the town so in December 1849 a meeting was held to discuss the matter and it was decided to form a company to build one. Shareholders included many of the Bradford wool barons such as Samuel Cunliffe Lister, Robert Milligan, and Titus Salt through whose influence the site was acquired. The hall quickly became the centre for cultural activities in the town. Concerts, plays, lectures and political meetings were all held there on occasion. However, many people remember it primarily as a cinema. Films were first shown there as early as 1898 and it continued as a picture house until after the Second World War. It was acquired by the Borough Council in 1952 and today is used principally as a concert hall. The mezzanine level entrance on Bridge Street is a recent addition (by Philip Mawson) which enhances the overall appearance of the building.

In the above photograph the Telegraph and Argus can be seen to the left of St George's Hall and the Victoria Hotel to the right. The hotel was built by a company formed by Sir Henry Ripley, the Bradford dyeing magnate, on a site adjoining Exchange Station. The station was considerably enlarged in the 1880's to become one of the finest in the country but it is one of the numerous Victorian masterpieces to have fallen to the demolishers. Other Bradford examples are the Swan Arcade and Kirkgate Market.

7. Theatre Royal (Manningham Lane; Andrews and Pepper, 1864)

Opening as the Royal Alexandra, the theatre was re-named in 1868 and passed through several hands until it was acquired in 1921 by the owner of the Alhambra, Francis Laidler. He sublet it as a cinema which it remained until 1976 when it finally closed. The most famous event in its history took place in 1905 when Sir Henry Irving, in the role of Becket, collapsed on stage after uttering the last words of the play, "Into thy hands, O Lord". He died the same evening in the foyer of the Midland Hotel, accompanied by Bram Stoker, his manager and the author of 'Dracula'.

8. and 9. Alhambra Theatre (Morley Street; Chadwick and Watson, 1914)

The 1800-seat Alhambra was built as a music hall for Francis Laidler who already owned the nearby Prince's Theatre (1876; 2,680 seats) which, with the adjacent Palace (1875; 1,200 seats), stood approximately where the National Museum of Film, Photography and Television stands today. The two photographs of the Alhambra give some indication of the very extensive redevelopment (The Renton Howard Wood Levin Partnership, 1986) which has greatly improved the theatre's facilities and arguably its appearance also.

8

9

10. and 11. The Old Post Office, now St Peter's House (Forster Square; Tanner, 1887)
The first record of a Post Office in Bradford was in the reign of Queen Anne; in 1705 William
Rawson, a local attorney, contracted for the delivery of letters between London and Tadcaster
and a number of other northern towns. It was then situated at the back of the Manor Hall but it
moved numerous times over the next one hundred and fifty years before moving into the old
Exchange Rooms in 1867. However, the volume of business was such that larger premises were
soon required and this led to the erection of the magnificent building, designed by Sir Henry

Tanner, which is seen above before and after restoration. The building of the Post Office, flanked by warehouses and the Midland Station, and the clearing of the area between Well Street and Broadstones, gave Bradford a fine open square which has since disappeared through redevelopment. We are fortunate that the Post Office at least has been saved. The contractors were J. and W. Beanland of Harris Street who were also responsible for building Exchange Station, the Swan Arcade and Lister's Mill, as well as York Barracks, Leeds Infirmary and All Saints Church, Halifax.

12. The National Westminster Bank (Hustlergate; Andrews and Pepper, 1868)
The Bradford Commercial Bank was founded in 1833. Its first office was in Market Street in the
building which had previously housed the Bradford Banking Company, established in 1827, and
Wentworth and Company which had failed in 1825. In 1868 it moved into its fine Gothic
premises in Hustlergate, merging in 1904 with the Bradford District Bank and in 1918 with the
National Provincial.

13. The Yorkshire Penny Bank (North Parade; Ledingham, 1893)

The Yorkshire Penny Bank, now the Yorkshire Bank, owes its existence to Edward Akroyd of Halifax, an industrialist and philanthropist who developed the model industrial community of Akroydon which has similarities with Saltaire. He wanted to encourage the habit of thrift among working men and in 1852 opened a Penny Bank for his workers. By 1859 he was able to extend the scheme throughout the region and the Yorkshire Penny Bank was started. There were 24 branches by the end of the year, operating from mechanics institutes, church halls, school rooms and even on occasion from pubs. The first conventional branch premises were opened in Leeds in 1865 and a full time branch opened in Manchester Road, Bradford, in 1872. The richly decorated building in North Parade is a measure of how successful the business had become by the 1890's.

14. and 15. Bradford and Ilkley Community College: Alexandra Annexe (Great Horton Road; Andrews and Pepper, 1879)
The Alexandra Hotel was built by a group of local businessmen. Shortly before the end of the century the Empire Music Hall was erected at the rear with an entrance through the hotel. This 'palatial hall of variety' prospered from 1899 until the opening of the Alhambra, then in 1916 it

became a venue for touring theatre. The stage was destroyed by fire the following year and from 1918 it was a cinema until 1952 when a further fire led to its closure and, in due course, the demolition of the auditorium. The hotel itself closed down and was taken over by Bradford College in 1972.

16. Midland Hotel (Cheapside; Trubshaw, 1885)
In 1874 the Midland Railway Company acquired land adjacent to its station and ten years later began to build a new station and adjoining hotel. The railway companies had recently rejected as unworkable the suggestion of connecting the Midland and Exchange stations. Trubshaw was the Midland Railway's chief architect. The new station opened in March 1890 and was renamed Bradford Forster Square in 1924.

17. The Registry Office (Manor Row; Andrews and Pepper, 1877)
The Registry was originally the offices of the Poor Law Union. However, the Clerk to the Board of Guardians was also the Superintendent Registrar and the building has always provided a room where marriages can take place.

18. Law Russell (Vicar Lane; Lockwood and Mawson, 1873)
This is one of Britain's outstanding Victorian warehouses, built in just nineteen months for Law, Russell and Co. by Archibald Neil, a pioneer of improved building techniques and a model employer. John Russell and John Douglas, originally both drapers, founded the home trade house of Russell, Douglas and Co. in 1837 and later occupied Robert Milligan's old premises in Kirkgate and Piccadilly. James Law joined the firm in 1842 as a bookkeeper and rose to become the senior partner.

19. Devere House (Vicar Lane; Lockwood and Mawson, 1871)
This export warehouse was constructed for Thornton, Homan and Company, shipping and commission agents who had a vast trade with China and the United States. The eagle over the entrance and the medallion motif of stars and stripes over the first floor windows reflect this American connection. The building is sometimes referred to as the American and Chinese Export Warehouse.

21. Little Germany

Austral House, Devere House and Law Russell are just three among many warehouses in the area known today as Little Germany. The first German immigrants came to Bradford in the 1820's and 1830's, mainly from the north, and included Jacob Behrens and Leo Schuster. More arrived after the 1870 Franco-Prussian War which interfered badly with trade between the two countries. These new Bradfordians not only quickly established themselves as an important merchant group but also supported many cultural institutions, such as the Bradford Festival Choral Society, and philanthropic enterprises. Charles Semon from Danzig, for example, helped to build and maintain several hospitals and he was elected the first foreign-born Mayor of Bradford. Jacob Moser launched a £10,000 Benevolent Fund for the aged and infirm workpeople of the town. The area most associated with the German community is Little Germany where there was an enormous expansion of warehousing for the storage of piece yarns, and to some extent wool, in the 1860's and early 1870's. This was as a consequence of the stimulus to trade given by the French commercial treaty of 1860.

In the photograph above, the building reflected in the puddle is Albion House (Hick Street and Vicar Lane; Milnes and France, 1868), where Kessler's became one of the first firms to export tops and noils to America at the end of the nineteenth century.

20. Austral House (Well Street)

This elaborately decorated building at 49-53 Well Street was probably designed by Eli Milnes and opened in the late 1860's. For many years it was used by Stavert, Zigmata and Co., stuff merchants, who were one of the many European companies who did so much to develop this area of the town. The architectural historian, John Ayers, has written of Austral House that "as an example of exuberant application of the craftsman's skills it has few peers."

22. Lister's Mill (Heaton Road, Andrews and Pepper, 1873)
Probably the most imposing mill in Bradford, Manningham Mills was built for Samuel Cunliffe
Lister and was the biggest silk mill in the world. The Heaton Road frontage was 350 yards, that on
Lilycroft Road 150 yards and the floor area extended to sixteen acres. The chimney stack is 249
feet high. It is said that Lister climbed the chimney on its completion and, breaking a bottle of
champagne, named it Lister's Pride.

23. Buttershaw Mill (Halifax Road; 1852)

James Bottomley and his two brothers began in business at Shelf employing several hand weavers. In 1844 they moved to Brighouse and later to Victoria Mills in Low Moor where they became worsted manufacturers. They erected the first part of Buttershaw Mill in 1852 and expanded into mohair and alpaca. Numerous cottages were built nearby, as was James Bottomley's own home, Farfield House. The mill's most famous employee was the engineer Joseph Hobson Jagger who put his expertise to good use when he visited Monte Carlo in 1875 and analysed the gearing of the roulette wheel in the Casino. He then started to bet and won two million francs in eight days. The writer, Fred Gilbert, heard of Jagger's exploits and wrote the famous song "The Man who Broke the Bank at Monte Carlo". Jagger returned to Bradford and is buried at Shelf.

24. The New Mill, Saltaire (Lockwood and Mawson, 1868)

Titus Salt was one of the most successful of the Bradford manufacturers, making his fortune by developing the use of alpaca as a raw material in the worsted trade. He became Mayor and was elected Member of Parliament.

In 1850 he started to build a modern industrial complex on a green field site. It was on the banks of the River Aire three miles from Bradford and he named it Saltaire. All his scattered industrial buildings were to be centralised in one place and there was to be a new village for his employees. His motives were mixed. The site was a good one for his business, having good communications with his markets and raw materials. He was ambitious to establish an industrial dynasty to compete with landed wealth and Saltaire was to be the centre of his empire. He was also genuinely concerned with improving the conditions of the workers.

Saltaire was to be a model, a practical example of how to achieve social and industrial harmony within a pleasant environment whilst retaining a hierarchical and deferential social system. The architecture reflects this ideal. Thus the buildings which express the authority of the master, such as the mill, the church and the institute, dominate the village. The hospital and almshouses are in the Gothic style indicating the values of rural England. Other buildings are in the Italian style reflecting, as one authority puts it, "the aggressive individualism of early Italian capitalism".

25. Albert Terrace, Saltaire, and Saltaire Mill (Lockwood and Mawson and Sir William Fairbairn, 1853)
The campanile-style chimney of the original mill is 250 feet tall.

26. Bolton Road warehouses (Demolished)

At the bottom of what would have been a typical Victorian Bradford ginnel, with its stone setts, paving slabs and dour warehouses, is the Ring O' Bells pub, the only building in this photograph to be still standing. Charles Semon had a warehouse here, and in this century the tramways offices were housed in the building which had earlier accommodated G. Harrison, 'steam printer'. Fortunately many other warehouses at the foot of Bolton Road and Canal Road still survive, among them the extensive premises occupied by the Empire Stores mail-order business. Both Empire Stores and Grattans were founded by members of the Fattorini family and have contributed significantly to the economic health of the city.

27. Black Dyke Mills (Queensbury; 1835 onwards)

Unlike Saltaire, Black Dyke Mills was not developed to a grand plan. John Foster started building on the site in 1835 and made additions as and when necessary: by 1865 it contained thirteen acres of floor space and employed some 3,500 workers. Nor did the Fosters build the village of Queensbury in the same way as Salt did Saltaire. Nevertheless they exercised almost as much influence through the community's economic dependence upon Black Dyke, causing the historian William Cudworth to remark after a visit to Queensbury that "it would be difficult to find a commmunity so thoroughly imbued with the spirit of their employer".

28 — 31. Preston Street Landscapes: City Road Goods Yard and Alston Works

The City Road goods yard was built by the Great Northern Railway Company in 1876 to serve the very busy industrial district around Thornton Road. There was a

private siding to Isaac Holden's Alston Works (Milnes and France, 1866) which can be seen in the earlier photographs above. The yard closed in 1972.
One of the important surviving mills is Daniel Illingworth & Sons' Whetley Mills (Thornton Road; Milnes and France, 1865).

32. Back-to-back housing (Preston Street/St Andrew's Villas)

These are superior examples of back-to-backs, the most common type of working class houses built during the nineteenth century. In the 1850's they accounted for about three quarters of all houses in the town and by the turn of the century some 40,000 back-to-backs housed two-thirds of the working population. A bye-law of 1860 had attempted to prevent any more being built but the council was forced to reverse its decision in the face of fierce opposition. The quality was improved, however, with better standards of light, ventilation and construction, and towards the end of the century there was increased provision for water closets and baths. Many Bradfordians still live in back-to-backs.

33. Terraced housing
Terraced houses such as these were usually the homes of the upper working and lower middle classes. Although they were often built next to or near back-to-backs, a social distinction might be drawn between the occupants of the two types of housing. Similarly, differences within housing types expressed and conferred degrees of social rank so that, for example, the standing of a household with a bay window would be higher than that of one without.

34. Semi-detached housing (Oakroyd Villas)

Bradford was noted for its lack of rigid segregation between the housing of the social classes and the various levels within them. This resulted both from its valley location and also because in expanding it had absorbed a number of old village centres such as Undercliffe which themselves contained various house types and social levels. Finally the only place free from industrial development was Manningham in which the 1861 census recorded the erection of "many houses of a superior class occupied by the principal families of the district." Oakroyd Villas are fine examples of the kind of middle class housing being built in the second half of the nineteenth century.

35. Bradford Tradesmens Homes (Lily Croft; 1868 and 1878)

The Bradford Tradesmen's Benevolent Institution was established in 1857 with the object of providing tradespeople who had fallen into poverty with the means of subsistence. Men were allowed £24 a year and women £18. In 1867 the Institute decided to extend its activities by building a number of almshouses and thirty were built the following year and a further thirteen in 1878.

36. St Luke's Hospital (Little Horton Lane; Lockwood and Mawson, 1852)
St Luke's originated as the Bradford Union Workhouse, housing some of the poorest
members of the community. Work began in 1850 and additions to Lockwood and
Mawson's original buildings, completed in 1852, were made over the next fifty years.
During the First World War it was a military hospital and in 1921 St Luke's became
the first municipal hospital in the country.

37. Rimmington's (Bridge Street; 1870)

Rimmington's is one of the oldest chemists in Bradford, Felix Rimmington of Ivegate appearing as a chemist and druggist as early as 1845. In the 1870's the firm moved to Bridge Street and also had a shop in Manningham Lane. The family lived in Manningham, in Eldon Terrace, near a number of other middle class manufacturers and professional people. By the twentieth century they had expanded into the aerated water business and were also manufacturing chemicals at a factory in Thorncliffe Road. The shop in Bridge Street remains, although it has recently been modernised.

38. Gray's Fisheries (Demolished)

Fish and chips are a traditional British meal and Yorkshire still has many shops and restaurants, such as Harry Ramsden's in Guiseley, which specialise in the dish. What made Gray's remarkable was its connection with Percy Shaw who invented the 'cat's-eyes' reflecting studs which are now a permanent feature on most roads. The friendship between Shaw and the shopkeeper led to the sign being made out of cat's-eyes which made it especially visible to passing motor traffic. The building was recently demolished to make way for a new ring road.

39. The Dudley Hill Picture House (Tong Street; 1912)

A purpose-built cinema, the Dudley Hill Picture House opened in 1912 with the film 'How's Your Father?' and was operated for over fifty years by members of the same family, the Goodalls. It closed with the film 'Thunderbirds Are Go' in 1967 to re-open as a bingo hall.

In the years before 1914 cinema-going was becoming an increasingly popular pastime and the trend continued between the wars. By 1940 there were forty-two picture houses in the town and many of them were located in the suburbs, making picture-going a local community activity. These suburban cinemas were often surprisingly large: Dudley Hill, for example, had seating for six hundred. There were still forty cinemas in 1950 but the advent first of television and latterly of video has reduced the present number of screens in Bradford to single figures.

40. The Cock and Bottle (Barkerend Road; original building eighteenth century; 1863 extensions by Richard Horsfall)

The classic Victorian pub developed during the third quarter of the nineteenth century. The use of the hand pump rather than the jug, and the emergence of the counter, began as early as 1800. Later, pubs evolved separate rooms for different functions. Thus there would be smoke rooms, commercial rooms, music rooms, the snug and the dram shop. Dram shops specialised in the sale of spirits and were often elaborately lit and decorated, though with minimal seating to encourage steady drinking. Pubs became increasingly luxurious, with decorated plate glass, embossed wall paper, large mirrors and paintings. The Cock and Bottle still displays many of the aspects of a typical Victorian pub, although it is much older. There is a record of a licence being granted as early as 1773 and the building may date back to at least 1747. The Otley Road turnpike was laid out in the 1820's and it may be that the Cock and Bottle was rebuilt to take advantage of the increased traffic passing its doors. In 1863 there were further alterations and additions.

41. The last delivery

42. The last lunchtime

41-44. The Moulders Arms (Demolished)

There is a reference to a licence being given to the Moulders Arms in 1827, though the pub may have been much older. It was used for social and political activities as well as by local ironworkers who held trade union and friendly society meetings in its

43. Boarded up

44. Demolition

rooms. In 1835, for example, 67 people had an 'excellent dinner' in its rooms to celebrate an election victory. It was eventually bought by Stocks Brewery of Shibden Head who were taken over by Webster's in 1933. In 1982 the Moulders was closed down in controversial circumstances.

45. Cartwright Hall (North Park Road; Simpson and Allen, 1904)

In 1870 Samuel Cunliffe Lister sold his fifty-three acre estate in Manningham to the council for use as a public park. In 1899 a competition was held to design a new art gallery to be built there and the foundation stone was laid the following year: the building was opened by Lister himself, by then Lord Masham, in 1904.

Samuel Cunliffe Lister (1815-1906) was one of the greatest Bradford textile magnates. The essential work of combing wool was done by hand until the 1840's when Lister and a Leeds engineer, G.E. Donisthorpe, designed a machine to do the job. Lister protected the invention by purchasing over twenty other patent rights and then monopolised the market. By the 1850's he was a wealthy man, but his energy was then directed to utilising silk waste and weaving silk velvet. Again he produced a successful machine and made a second fortune.

46. Bradford and Ilkley Community College: Old Building (Great Horton Road; Hope and Jardine, 1882)

As early as 1852 the Mayor, William Rand, a leading manufacturer, organised a meeting to discuss the establishment of a school of design in the town but nothing came of the proposal. It was resurrected in 1868 during a great national debate on Britain's educational system and Bradford MP W.E. Forster urged the Chamber of Commerce to recommend the establishment of a Technical College. However it was to be another ten years before such a project was undertaken. Despite the difficult gradient, the architects designed a magnificent building which the Prince of Wales opened as the Technical School in 1882.

47. University of Bradford Management Centre (Emm Lane; Lockwood and Mawson, 1877)

The building was constructed to rehouse Airedale College, an institution then based in Undercliffe which originated in an academy for Congregationalist ministers established in Heckmondwike in 1756. In 1888 it became the United Independent College.

48. Bowling Back Lane Board School (Demolished; Milnes and France, 1874)

Bowling Back Lane was the first of a group of eight purpose-built elementary schools to be opened in Bradford to meet the requirements of the 1870 Education Act introduced by Bradford MP W.E. Forster. The Bradford Observer described the completed building as 'really splendid' both architecturally and educationally. It was provided with large and lofty rooms and each had a large open fireplace as well as central heating. There was accommodation for 584 pupils and whilst only 156 were admitted on the first day, attendance had risen to 842 by 1886. Although Bowling Back Lane has been demolished, other early elementary schools, such as Lilycroft (Hope and Jardine) and Barkerend (Andrews and Pepper), have fortunately survived.

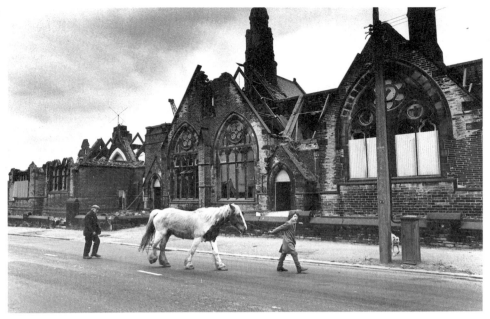

49. Pollard Park Middle School (Barkerend Road; Hargreaves, 1897)
Originally Hanson Higher Board School, the school took its name from James
Hanson who was a member of the Bradford School Board for twenty four years and
Chairman for six from 1888. Bradford had initiated classes beyond the elementary
stage as early as 1876: Hanson was a strong supporter of higher education and his
forceful and farseeing advocacy of this cause was a major factor in the building of this
school and of Belle Vue (Hargreaves, 1895).

50. St John's Church (Bowling; R.H. and S. Sharp, 1842)
John Wood was a well-known Bradford manufacturer and philanthropist. He was an ally of
Richard Oastler in the Ten Hours Movement and was responsible for the building of St James
Church (Manchester Road; Rawstorne, 1838). After it had been completed it is said he
reproached the Bowling Iron Company for failing to provide a church for their workforce and
that the company built St John's because they were stung by the criticism. Cast iron has similar
structural properties to masonry, and the architects, assisted by the works engineer, Fred Stott,
used it extensively for columns and arches.

51. All Saints' Church (Little Horton Green; Thomas, T.H. and F. Healey, 1864)
In 1859 the Bradford Church Building Society was formed with the aim of increasing provision
for Anglican worship in the town. Not only was the population growing but the 1851 religious
census had shown that Bradford was nonconformist rather than Anglican. The Society decided to
build ten new churches and this programme was completed by 1872. The finest of these churches
is All Saints'. The site was provided by Mr (later Sir) Francis Sharp Powell of Horton Old Hall, a
Conservative M.P and philanthropist, who also met the costs of construction.

52. Sion Baptist Chapel (Harris Street; Lockwood and Mawson, 1873)

In the middle of the nineteenth century the principal Baptist centres were Birmingham, Bristol and Bradford. The original Sion Chapel, built in 1823, stood in Bridge Street on a site which was sold to the Lancashire and Yorkshire Railway Company after the opening of the new chapel. The minister responsible for the move was J.P. Chown, who was as prominent in Bradford life as his most distinguished predecessor, Benjamin Godwin.

53. Sheikhs Restaurant (Simes Street; 1849)

The building was formerly St Andrew's Presbyterian Church. The first minister, the Rev. Alexander Wallace, stayed in Bradford for only three years but succeeded in attracting a large congregation during that time. The church was popular with Bradford's significant Scottish community and was known as the Scotch Church.

54. Eastbrook Hall (Leeds Road; W.J. Morley and Son, 1903)

A Methodist Society was formed in Bradford in the middle of the eighteenth century and in 1766 an octagonal "preaching-house", demolished in 1950, was built in Great Horton Road. In 1825 Eastbrook Chapel was erected to a simple Gothic design amid fears that the site was too far removed from the town. It was replaced in 1903 by Eastbrook Hall which, behind a flat facade, revived the octagonal form favoured by John Wesley. Uncertainty caused by the drift of congregations to the suburbs and the conversion of wealthier nonconformist patrons to Anglicanism was reflected in the incorporation of shops into the Leeds Road frontage to provide additional revenue. A buyer for the building is currently being sought.

53

54

55. and 56. Undercliffe Cemetery
The buildings have now been demolished. Entering from Undercliffe Lane, the site of the registrar's house is to the right and of the sexton's lodge to the left.

Undercliffe Cemetery (Undercliffe Lane and Otley Road; laid out by William Gay, 1854)
The Bradford Cemetery Company bought twenty six acres of land at Undercliffe in 1851 and subsequently appointed William Gay, registrar of Leicester Cemetery, to be the first registrar and design the layout. Unlike pre-industrial church yards where the wealthy and powerful were buried next to the poor, Undercliffe was divided into areas which were governed by a scale of charges ranging from £3 to £10 per grave plot. Thus wealth determined where you were buried. Joseph Smith, a land surveyor, allocated and divided the plots in terms of accessibility and view.

His own plot is probably the finest in the cemetery: his thirty foot monument overlooks central Bradford and is visible from many parts of the city. The remoter areas of the cemetery were allocated to those who could not afford their own grave and their coffins were buried several deep. Over 123,000 internments were to take place before the Company went into voluntary liquidation in the mid 1970's. Following a period of neglect and vandalism, a new company was formed with the support of the council to administer and promote the cemetery as a place of historical importance and to ensure its continuation as a place of burial.

57. Undercliffe Cemetery
The 1878 mortuary chapels, Anglican and nonconformist, have now been demolished. They were designed by Lockwood and Mawson and replaced the original chapels of Mallinson and Healey.

58. Undercliffe Cemetery
A view along the main promenade towards the obelisk commemorating Joseph Smith (1801-1858).

59. Undercliffe Cemetery: the Illingworth Mausoleum

Daniel Illingworth (1772-1854) founded what became one of the largest spinning businesses in Bradford, taking his sons Alfred and Henry into partnership with him and marrying them to daughters of Isaac Holden (1807-1897), the notable Bradford businessman, inventor and employer. Illingworth's daughter Margaret married Holden's eldest son, Angus, subsequently Lord Holden of Alston (1833-1912). The mausoleum was erected to the memory of Alfred Illingworth (1827-1907) who was a prominent politician as well as a major figure in the worsted trade. Daniel and Henry are buried nearby, as is Sir Isaac Holden.

60. Undercliffe Cemetery: the Swithen Anderton and Atkinson Jowett memorials

Swithen Anderton (1803-1860) was a woolstapler, magistrate, and a leading figure in the town. His memorial is based on the Scott Monument in Princes Street, Edinburgh. James Atkinson Jowett owned extensive estates in Yorkshire which were the subject of a celebrated law case during his father's lifetime. He was an alderman, a member of the Bradford Board of Guardians and a director of the Bradford Commercial Bank. He was also a generous supporter of the Church of England, endowing Bolton Parish Church, Bradford. He died in 1886 aged 69. Samuel Jackson designed the Italianate Grove House, Bolton, for him in 1860.

61. Undercliffe Cemetery: the Behrens family and Jonathan Holden memorials
The Baroque tablet commemorates members of the Behrens family, most notably Sir Jacob
Behrens (1806-1889). The son of a Hamburg merchant, he moved to Bradford in 1838 and made
his fortune in the export trade. He helped found the Bradford Chamber of Commerce, took an
active role in the development of educational provision and was a notable philanthropist. The
Graeco-Roman temple commemorates Jonathan Holden (1828-1906), a relative of Sir Isaac.

62. Undercliffe Cemetery: the central area during restoration

63. Undercliffe Cemetery: the main promenade

64. Undercliffe Cemetery: a social encounter

65. Undercliffe Cemetery: the Joseph Smith memorial

Alphabetical Index of the Photographs